LIFE INSURANCE

THE GIFT OF LIFE AFTER LIFE

Author/Editor: Rev. Darryl Bass

Electronic ISBN: 978-1-972115-20-6 (EPUB),
978-1-972115-75-6 (Kindle)
Paperback ISBN: 978-1-972115-21-3
Hardcover ISBN: 978-1-972115-22-0
Printed in the United States

The Library of Congress Control Number: 2026905819

Bass Publishing, LLC
Maywood, IL 60153

Disclaimer

Scripture quotations are taken from the King James Version of the Bible.

About the Author

Meet the visionary behind "The Life Progression System," Reverend Darryl Bass. From his tenure at Citibank to his current role as Assistant Pastor at Impact Church in Maywood, IL, Darryl's journey as a life, financial, and spiritual coach epitomizes determination and unwavering faith.

For more than two decades, Darryl has been joined in marriage to his steadfast partner, Patricia. Their enduring union stands as a testament to the values he cherishes. As a devoted father to nine children—Darnisha, Darryl Jr., Wardell, Darrell, Candance, Tyanne, Cierra, Cayleen, and John—he imparts his wisdom to future generations, leaving behind a legacy of love, strength, and commitment.

Darryl's entrepreneurial spirit shines through his various ventures. Founding Divine and Righteous Solutions, Divine Debt Solutions, Righteous Rewards, Savings Solutions, 4MyDebt Solutions, Divine and Righteous Realty, and collaborating with his wife in Divine Delights and Clara's Kitchen, he paints a picture of success across diverse domains.

Always forward-thinking, Darryl is pioneering a transformative course to liberate individuals from the burdens of debt. His holistic approach encompasses credit building, income growth, robust savings, and secure retirement planning—while also nurturing families and building legacies for generations. His commitment to giving back is evident through his emphasis on tithing, a cornerstone of his belief in abundance.

With steadfast dedication, Reverend Darryl Bass answers the divine call to create abundance for all who seek it and to lead an Exodus from the bondage of debt, freeing individuals from the chains of indebtedness. He stands as a beacon of possibility. His life's work, encapsulated within the pages of "The Life Progression System," illuminates a path toward personal, financial, and spiritual elevation. Join us in honoring a journey fueled by purpose, perseverance, and an unwavering commitment to enrich lives.

Acknowledgements

First, I acknowledge **God**, the Giver of Life, Wisdom, Vision, and Purpose.

The One who teaches us that stewardship is worship, and preparation is an act of love.

Without Him, none of this would exist.
To Him be the glory forever.

To my wife and my family — thank you for your patience, your encouragement, your prayers, and your unwavering belief in the calling on my life. Every dream is easier to carry when love is holding it with you.

To my spiritual covering, mentors, and leaders who have poured into me — thank you for shaping my character, sharpening my discernment, and reinforcing that excellence is a requirement, not an option.

To the families, clients, students, and individuals who have entrusted me with your financial journeys — thank you for giving me the honor of walking with you. Your courage to break generational cycles inspired every word of this book.

To every person who has ever struggled financially and thought, *"There has to be more to life than this,"* you were right — and I pray this book helps you see that more clearly than ever before.

Finally, to every reader holding this book:
May your life be changed.
May your family be strengthened.
May your legacy be established.
And may generations you will never meet rise up and call you blessed.

Because of the decisions you make today, someone you love will live better tomorrow.

And that — is the gift of life after life.

Dedication

To every mother who stretched,
every father who endured,
every grandparent who sacrificed,
every caregiver who did the best they could with what they had.

To those who taught us to pray,
but were never taught how to plan.
To those who kept the family together,
even when life was falling apart.

To the ones who worked hard,
loved hard,
gave everything they had—
and yet had nothing left to leave behind.

This book is dedicated to you.

And to every child, son, daughter, niece, nephew, grandchild, and future descendant who deserves to inherit more than struggle—

you are the reason we change the narrative.
You are the reason we build differently.
You are the reason we plan forward.

This is for the next generation.
This is for legacy.
This is for life — after life.

— Rev. Darryl Bass

Foreword

Most people think life insurance is about death. But the truth is — **life insurance is about life.**

It is about the life your family will live *after* you are no longer here to protect them, guide them, or provide for them. It is about honor. It is about stewardship. It is about love that prepares in advance.

For too long, life insurance has been misunderstood, ignored, feared, or dismissed. Many of us grew up in environments where financial survival was the only priority. We were taught how to get by — not how to build. We were told to **work**, not to **prepare**. We learned how to manage bills, not how to establish legacy.

And as a result, generation after generation has been forced to start from scratch.

But what if we could end that cycle — permanently?

This book is not simply about policies and premiums. It is not a sales pitch, a product manual, or an industry brochure.
This book is **revelation.**
This book is **course correction.**
This book is **a blueprint for generational transformation.**

Rev. Darryl Bass writes with clarity, compassion, and conviction. He does not speak as a theorist, but as a shepherd of families, a leader of households, a coach of communities, and a voice to the generations. He understands that wealth is not first about money — it is about **mindset, identity, and intentionality.**

He breaks down life insurance in a way that **anyone can understand**, yet **everyone can value** — from the financially inexperienced to the investment-savvy. He exposes myths, clarifies confusion, and brings forward the truth that has been hidden behind fear, misinformation, and cultural silence.

What you are holding in your hands is **a gift** — one that your children and grandchildren may one day thank you for.

This book will help you:

- See money differently
- Understand responsibility differently
- Love your family differently
- Protect your legacy differently

And most of all, it will help you leave behind something much greater than memories:

A future.

If you read this book with an open mind and a willing spirit, you will not just gain knowledge — you will gain strategy. You will gain clarity. You will gain the peace that comes from knowing your family will always be covered.

This is **not** just about preparing for death.
This is about **empowering life — after life.**

And that, my friend — is love in its highest form.

Introduction — Why This Book Matters — Right Now

Most people don't struggle financially because they are irresponsible, undisciplined, or unmotivated.
They struggle because they were never taught how money actually works. We were raised in households where the priority was **survival, not structure**. We learned how to stretch, endure, make it through, pray, and "make something out of nothing." But we were not taught how to build, multiply, preserve, or transfer wealth.

So we grew up thinking **hard work was the key** — never realizing that **hard work without structure only produces exhaustion**.

And when it comes to life insurance, many people are living with a misunderstanding so deep that it has affected entire generations.

We were taught that life insurance is:

Something you buy when you're old.

Something you only use when you die.

Something mysterious, complicated, or unnecessary.

"Death insurance."

But life insurance **is not about death** — it is about **life.**

It is about protecting **your family's life** after yours ends.
It is about ensuring they **don't lose everything when they lose you.**
It is about love that speaks **after your voice is gone.**

And for many families, this is the **difference between generational struggle and generational stability.**

A Moment That Changed Everything

I will never forget the phone call I received one night.

A father had passed suddenly.
Hard worker. Provider. Protector.
He was the strength of the family — emotionally, spiritually, financially.

But there was **no life insurance.**

And as the family was grieving the loss of the man they loved…
they were also:

Meeting with funeral directors

Negotiating costs, they couldn't afford

Trying to raise money in group chats

Planning car washes and GoFundMe campaigns

Arguing about who could contribute what

Pain became pressure.
Grief became crisis.
Loss became embarrassment.

And I remember thinking:

This should not be happening.

Not in our families.
Not in our communities.
Not in our generation.

We cannot keep **mourning publicly and scrambling privately.**

There is a **better way.**
A **simple way.**
A **wise way.**
A **legacy-building way.**

And that way is **life insurance.**

The Truth No One Told Us

Life insurance is **not just a policy.**
It is a:

- Financial strategy
- Generational asset
- Wealth transfer tool

- Stability guarantee
- Love letter to your family's future

When done correctly:

- It pays off mortgages
- It funds college educations
- It eliminates debt
- It sustains the household income
- It prevents financial collapse
- It creates inheritance
- It builds generational wealth *tax-free*

This is not about **preparing for death.**
It's about **protecting their life.**

This Book Will Teach You How to:

- Understand every major type of life insurance
- Know which policy fits each stage of life
- Avoid being over-insured, under-insured, or misinformed
- Build wealth with cash value policies

- Protect your family from emergency-based decision-making
- Transfer wealth intentionally and strategically

You will learn how to **use life insurance the way the wealthy do — not the way the average person has been taught.**

Because while we have been taught to **work for money,**
the wealthy use life insurance to **make money work for them and their families — forever.**

The Shift Begins Here

By the time you finish this book, you will:

- Understand insurance
- Feel confident choosing the right policy
- Know how to protect your family at every life stage
- And have the blueprint to build and transfer generational wealth

This is more than education.
This is transformation.
This is restoration.
This is legacy.

Let's build something that **outlives us**.

Let's give our families the greatest gift we can:

Life — after life.

Section One: Insurance Basics

Chapter 1 — Debunking the Myth #1: Not Death Insurance, But Life Insurance

Some people say:
"Why should I pay for life insurance? I won't be here to use it."

And that statement right there reveals the misunderstanding.

Life insurance is not about the person who passes — it's for the people who remain.

It is not "death insurance."
It is **love insurance.**
It is **responsibility insurance.**
It is **legacy insurance.**

It says:
"I may not be here physically, but my love, my

provision, my support, and my protection will still be present."

If your family depends on your income to live today,
they will depend on your insurance to live tomorrow.

Because bills won't stop.
Rent won't stop.
Groceries won't stop.
Life will still need to be lived.

And without life insurance, your family is left to:

Sell what you owned

Rely on donations

Lose the home

Live in struggle

Start over in pain and confusion

Life insurance prevents that.
It protects your family from emotional grief becoming financial disaster.

Chapter 2 — Why You Need Life Insurance

You need life insurance if:

- Someone depends on your income
- You have children
- You have a mortgage
- You have debt
- You love your family
- You want to leave a legacy
- You desire dignity in your final arrangements
- You refuse to let your family struggle financially in your absence

This is **not just financial planning.**
This is **love in action.**

When we die without insurance:

- Our family is left to figure out costs.
- They may be forced to choose between grieving and survival.

- They may lose stability right when life hurts the most.

Life insurance says:
"When I can't be here to protect you — the protection is still here."

It is one of the **most selfless, honorable, loving decisions** a person can make.

Chapter 3 — Understanding the Types of Life Insurance

Here are the major types, explained simply and clearly:

1. Term Life Insurance

- Coverage for a set amount of time (10, 20, or 30 years)
- **Affordable + High coverage**
- Best for income replacement and protecting young families

2. Whole Life Insurance

- Lifetime coverage
- Builds **cash value** you can borrow from
- More expensive, but **wealth-building**

3. Universal Life (UL)

- Lifetime coverage
- Flexible premiums

- Cash value grows based on interest rates

4. Indexed Universal Life (IUL)

- Cash value grows based on **market index performance**
- **Upside potential with downside protection**
- Great for retirement and wealth building

5. Variable Universal Life (VUL)

- Cash value invested in the market
- Higher risk, higher reward
- Best for confident investors

6. Guaranteed Universal Life (GUL)

- Lifetime coverage with **low cost**
- Little to no cash value
- Pure protection

7. Final Expense / Burial Insurance

- Small whole life policy for seniors

- Covers funeral and end-of-life costs
- Prevents family burden

8. Mortgage Life Insurance

- Pays off mortgage upon death
- **But the bank gets the money, not your family**
- Usually better to use Term Life instead

9. Key Person Insurance

- Protects a business or ministry if a crucial leader passes

10. Buy-Sell Agreement Insurance

- Ensures smooth transfer of business ownership upon death

11. Child / Juvenile Whole Life

- Insures children at extremely low rates
- Locks in coverage for life
- Builds wealth they can use later

12. Survivorship / Second-to-Die

- Covers two people, usually a married couple
- Pays out after both pass
- Used for **generational wealth + estate planning**

Now in the section to follow, we will go more in depth in the details of each of these types of insurances, but before we do that I need to discuss one thing and that is the whole dilemma about **whole vs term.** So in the next chapter, I will explain my position on it!

Chapter 4 — Whole Life vs Term Life: Ending the Confusion, Misunderstanding, and Mis-teaching

Why the Debate Exists, What Each Side Gets Right, What Each Side Gets Wrong, and Why the Truth is Not Either/Or — It's Both.

The Controversy

For decades, people have argued:

- **"Buy Term and Invest the Difference!"**
  vs.
- **"Whole Life is the only real wealth-building insurance!"**

And both sides swear they're right.
Both sides teach with passion.
Both sides think the other side is doing harm.

But the real truth?

They're both right — and they're both wrong. Because neither insurance type is "better." They simply serve *different purposes* at *different stages of life.*

This chapter will show the *complete truth.*

Where the Debate Started

In the 1970s and 80s:

- Banks changed how interest worked
- Employer pensions began disappearing
- The stock market became more accessible
- Financial authors began pushing **Term + Investing**

Books, TV personalities, and radio educators taught that:

Whole Life was too expensive,
and instead you should **buy cheap Term and invest the savings.**

It wasn't malicious.
But it was **incomplete**.

Because while Term is the **best protection**,
it does **not build wealth.**

And while Whole Life **builds wealth**,
it is **too expensive for some stages of life** to use alone.

So the debate didn't come from truth vs. lies.
It came from **truth vs. half-truth.**

The Case for Term Life Insurance

People who promote Term Life argue:

1. **It's affordable.**
   You can get a lot of coverage for a low price.

2. **It protects your family when they need protection most.**
   During your working and debt-paying years.
3. **It makes sure the household doesn't collapse if you die too young.**

And they are **right.**
Term Life is **the best tool** for:

- Young adults
- New parents
- People who are building income
- Families with rent/mortgages/debt
- Anyone whose death would crush their family financially

Term is **the shield**.

But here is where Term fails:

- It eventually **expires**
- It **builds no wealth**
- And if you outlive the policy — **your family gets nothing**

So Term **protects your family's present,**
but it **does not build your legacy's future.**

The Case for Whole Life

People who advocate Whole Life argue:

1. **Premiums stay the same forever.**
2. **Coverage lasts until you die — guaranteed.**
3. **It builds cash value that grows every year.**
4. **You can borrow against it for:
    - College
    - Retirement
    - Emergencies
    - Business capital
    - Home down payments**

And they are **right.**
Whole Life is **one of the greatest tools for generational wealth.**

Whole Life:

- **Builds wealth**
- **Creates inheritance**
- **Transfers wealth tax-free**
- **Becomes a personal bank system**

Whole Life **is the legacy builder.**

But here is where Whole Life fails:

- It **costs more**
- It is **harder to afford early in life**
- It can feel heavy if income is unstable

So Whole Life **builds your family's future,** but it **may be too expensive to protect your family's present *alone*.**

Here Is the Truth No One Talks About

It is **not:**

Term vs. Whole Life

The real formula is:

Term for the years your income must be replaced
Whole Life for the years your legacy must be established

They are **not enemies.**
They are **teammates.**
They are **sequential.**
They serve **different seasons.**

The Right Policy Depends on the Stage of Life

Stage of Life	Financial Reality	Best Insurance Strategy
0–18 (Childhood)	No income, identity development	**Child Whole Life**
18–25 (Launch)	Low income, new debt risks	**Convertible Term**
25–35 (Family Formation)	Income + mortgage + kids	**Large Term + Start Whole Life or IUL**

Stage of Life	Financial Reality	Best Insurance Strategy
35–55 (Wealth Building)	Highest income & responsibility	**Term + Expand Whole Life/IUL**
55–69 (Preservation)	Fewer dependents, retirement focus	**Whole Life or GUL + Single Premium Life**
69+ (Legacy)	Wealth transfer + funeral clarity	**Final Expense + Survivorship + Legacy Whole Life**

So the question is **never**:

"Which is better? Term or Whole Life?"

The real question is:

"What stage of life am I in, and what does my family need right now?"

Final Truth

Term Life **protects their today.**
Whole Life **protects their tomorrow.**

Term Life says:

"If I leave early, my family will not collapse."

Whole Life says:

"When I go, I will leave them prepared, provided for, and empowered."

Together, they say:

"My family will be protected in my absence and prosper in my memory."

This is not just insurance.
This is **spiritual stewardship.**
This is **financial maturity.**
This is **legacy leadership.**

This is how you:

- Break generational lack
- Build generational confidence
- And leave generational blessing

This is how you live intentionally and leave powerfully.

Section Two:
Insurance Types

Chapter 5 — Level Term Life Insurance

Protection During the Years You're Building, Growing, and Raising

What It Is

Level Term Life Insurance provides coverage for a set period of time — usually **10, 15, 20, 25, or 30 years** — where the **death benefit and premium remain the same** throughout the entire term.

This is the **simplest and most affordable** form of life insurance.
It is designed to protect your family through your **highest responsibility years** — when you are raising children, building a career, and paying off major expenses.

How It Works

You select:

- A **coverage amount** (e.g., $250,000, $500,000, $1,000,000)
- A **term length** (e.g., 20-year term)

You pay a **fixed premium** each month.

If you pass away during that period:

- Your beneficiary (usually spouse or children) receives the **full tax-free benefit.**

If you outlive the term:

- Coverage ends, unless you **renew**, **convert**, or **replace** the policy.

What It Is Used For

- Protecting **income** that supports your household

- Ensuring your family can maintain living standards if you pass
- Covering **major debts** (mortgage, car loans, tuition)
- Providing **financial security while you build wealth**

This is **financial protection**, not a savings plan.

Cost

Level Term is typically:

- The **lowest-cost** life insurance option
- Designed to fit family budgets
- Affordable even at high coverage amounts

Cost depends on:

- Age
- Health
- Lifestyle
- Term length
- Coverage amount

Example:
A healthy 35-year-old may pay:

- **$25–$45/month** for $500,000 in coverage

Pros

Strength	Impact
Affordable	High coverage without financial strain
Simple	Easy to understand and explain
Predictable Costs	Premium stays the same every month
Strong Family Protection	Replaces lost income during key earning years

Cons

Limitation	Impact
Coverage Ends	If you outlive the term, coverage may expire

Limitation	Impact
No Cash Value	Does not build savings or retirement funds
Premium Increases at Renewal	Renewing later in life can be costly

Who and When It Is Best For

Best for:

- Parents with young children
- Families with a mortgage
- People early in their financial journey
- Anyone needing **maximum protection at minimum cost**

Best Time to Get It:
As early as possible.
The younger and healthier you are, the lower your cost — **for the entire term.**

Encouragement

This policy says:

'My family's future is too important to leave uncertain."

It is **love in financial form**, expressed responsibly, wisely, and proactively.

Chapter 6 — Decreasing Term Life Insurance

Protection That Shrinks as Your Debt Shrinks

What It Is

Decreasing Term is a type of term insurance where the **death benefit decreases over time** — usually at the same pace as a **mortgage or other loan balance declines**.

Premiums typically stay level.

How It Works

- Coverage starts high (e.g., $300,000 mortgage)
- Each year, the benefit decreases
- Premium stays the same

- If you pass away during the term, the policy pays the **remaining debt amount**

This prevents your family from inheriting **major debt**, especially **a house payment.**

What It Is Used For

- **Mortgage protection**
- Car or personal loans
- Business loans
- Protecting co-signers from financial burden

This is not about leaving extra money.
This is about preventing **loss**.

Cost

- Usually **cheaper than Level Term**
- Because the payout **gets smaller every year**

Pros

Strength	Impact
Inexpensive	Lower cost than most insurance styles
Debt Protection	Ensures major debts are paid
Simple	Straightforward purpose and function

Cons

Limitation	Impact
Coverage Decreases	Benefit becomes smaller each year
No Wealth or Legacy Component	Protects the bank and home, not generational inheritance
No Cash Value	Not a financial growth tool

Who and When It Is Best For

Best for:

- People whose **main financial goal is keeping the home**

- Individuals who do not require income replacement
- Those with **limited budget** for insurance

Not Ideal for:

- Families who want to leave **additional** inheritance
- Anyone wanting **long-term legacy impact**

Encouragement

This is a **stability tool**, not a wealth tool.
It says:

"My family will not lose their home because I am no longer here."

And that is love, too.

Chapter 7 — Increasing Term Life Insurance

Coverage That Grows as Your Responsibilities Grow

What It Is

Increasing Term Life Insurance is term insurance where the **death benefit gradually increases** over time.
Some policies keep premiums level; others increase them to match the rising benefit.

This protects households whose **financial responsibilities are growing**, not shrinking.

How It Works

- You start with a base coverage amount (e.g., $200,000)

- Each year, coverage increases by a fixed percentage (often **3%–5% annually**)
- This growth helps combat:
    - **Inflation**
    - **Rising cost of living**
    - **Growing family needs**

What It Is Used For

- Young families planning for more children
- Households expecting income increases
- People concerned about inflation over time
- Protecting against **being underinsured later**

Cost

- More expensive than Level Term
- Less expensive than most Permanent policies

You are paying for **coverage that grows**, not coverage that shrinks.

Pros

Strength	Impact
Keeps Up with Inflation	Ensures coverage doesn't become outdated
Adapts to Life Changes	Matches increasing household responsibilities
Avoids Underinsurance	Expanding protection as income rises

Cons

Limitation	Impact
Premiums May Increase	Depending on policy design
More Expensive Than Level Term	Cost reflects growing benefit
No Cash Value	Not a wealth-building policy

Who and When It Is Best For

Best for:

- Young couples planning to expand family
- People expecting promotions, career growth, or business expansion
- Families who want to **stay ahead of rising costs**

Encouragement

This policy represents **growth mindset** and **forward-thinking stewardship**.

It says:

"I believe my life, my income, and my family's future are increasing — so my protection must increase as well."

Chapter 8 — Convertible Term Life Insurance

Short-Term Protection That Can Evolve into Life-Long Legacy

What It Is

Convertible Term Insurance is a term life policy that includes the option to **convert** some or all of the coverage into a **permanent life insurance policy without** a medical exam or proof of health later.

This means you can start with **low-cost protection**, and when you're ready, **upgrade** into wealth-building coverage — even if your health changes.

This is **financial foresight and strategic flexibility.**

How It Works

1. You buy a term policy.
2. The policy includes a **conversion privilege** that lasts for a set number of years.
3. During that period, you can convert the policy to:
   - **Whole Life**
   - **Universal Life**
   - **IUL (Indexed Universal Life)**
   - **GUL (Guaranteed Universal Life)**
4. When converting:
   - Your **health rating from the original application is locked in**
   - There is **no medical exam**
   - No new underwriting
   - No health questions

Meaning:

Even if you develop high blood pressure, diabetes, cancer, or any illness —
you cannot be denied the upgrade.

What It Is Used For

- Protecting family now while allowing for **wealth-building later**
- Ensuring future insurability
- Building legacy **step-by-step**
- Transitioning from income protection → generational wealth

Cost

Convertible Term costs the **same as regular term** with the added **conversion privilege** built in.

When you later convert:

- Your premiums **increase** because you are switching to a **permanent policy**
- But your **health rating is preserved**, which can save **thousands** in lifetime cost

Pros

Strength	Impact
Guaranteed Upgrade	Convert anytime within allowed period without a medical exam
Protects Against Health Changes	Future health issues cannot block coverage
Flexibility	Start low-cost, increase wealth-building when ready
Legacy-Ready	Enables long-term protection and inheritance

Cons

Limitation	Impact
Conversion Deadline	Must convert before the conversion window closes
Permanent Policies Cost More	Upgrade requires higher premium commitment
Requires Planning	Best used intentionally, not accidentally

Who & When It Is Best For

Best for:

- Young families building stability
- Entrepreneurs whose income will grow over time
- Individuals with **family medical history**
- Anyone who values **flexibility and future legacy planning**

Best Time to Get It:
When you want **full protection now**, and **wealth opportunity later**.

Encouragement

This policy says:

"My today may be limited — but my future will not be."

It is **faith-based planning** and **financial maturity in action.**

Chapter 9 — Renewable Term Life Insurance

The Safety Net Policy That Ensures Coverage Doesn't End When Life Changes

What It Is

Renewable Term Insurance allows you to **renew your term coverage** when the initial term ends **without** going through another medical exam.

Even if:

- Your health has changed
- You've aged significantly
- Your risk factors have increased

You are still guaranteed coverage.

How It Works

- You select a **term** (ex: 10, 20, 30 years)
- When it expires, you may **renew** the coverage
- **No medical exam. No underwriting. No health questions.**
- Premiums will increase due to age, but **you cannot be denied coverage**

This prevents you from being caught **uninsured** later in life.

What It Is Used For

- Protecting families while transitioning
- Covering gaps when permanent insurance isn't in place yet
- Keeping coverage active while income improves
- Maintaining dignity and protection in aging years

Cost

- Initially affordable (similar to standard term)
- Cost increases at renewal due to age
- Renewal is **not meant to last forever**, but as a **bridge strategy**

Pros

Strength	Impact
No Health Requirements to Renew	Health changes cannot cancel your coverage
Flexible	Extends protection during uncertain seasons
Peace of Mind	You are not left uncovered when term ends

Cons

Limitation	Impact
Premiums Increase After Renewal	Can become expensive later in life

Limitation	Impact
Still Temporary Coverage	Eventually needs to be replaced or converted
No Cash Value	Not a savings or wealth-building vehicle

Who & When It Is Best For

Best for:

- Those who want **security against the unexpected**
- People not yet ready to commit to permanent insurance
- Families in financial rebuilding phases
- Anyone concerned their health could change later

Encouragement

This policy is **your insurance parachute**.

It says:

"No matter what happens to my health, my family will not be left unprotected."

This is **wisdom + compassion + stewardship.**

Chapter 10 — Whole Life Insurance

The Foundation of Legacy: Protection + Cash Value + Generational Wealth

What It Is

Whole Life Insurance is a **permanent life insurance policy** that provides:

1. **Lifetime coverage**
2. A guaranteed **death benefit**
3. A **cash value** savings account that grows every year

This is the **classic**, time-tested wealth-building life insurance policy.

How It Works

Each premium payment is split:

- Part funds your death benefit
- Part goes into **cash value**, which:
  - Grows tax-deferred
  - Earns guaranteed interest
  - May earn dividends (with mutual insurance companies)
  - Can be borrowed against — **tax-free**

Cash value can be used to:

- Start a business
- Pay off debt
- Buy real estate
- Fund retirement
- Handle emergencies
- Finance college

This policy becomes **your family bank.**

What It Is Used For

- **Permanent protection**
- **Generational wealth transfer**
- **Retirement income supplementation**

- **Debt elimination strategy**
- **Financial stability and liquidity**
- **Estate and inheritance planning**

Cost

Whole Life has **higher premiums** because it does **more**:

- Protects
- Saves
- Grows
- Transfers wealth

Example:
A 35-year-old may pay:

- $120–$300/month for a strong Whole Life policy

But they are **buying ownership, not renting protection.**

Pros

Strength	Impact
Lifetime Coverage	Your protection never expires
Cash Value Growth	Tax-advantaged wealth that grows every year
Fixed Premiums	Cost never increases
Borrowing Power	You can use your policy as your own bank
Generational Legacy	Guarantees inheritance

Cons

Limitation	Impact
Higher Cost	Requires financial commitment
Slow Early Cash Growth	Wealth builds strongest over time
Not Designed for Short-Term Flip	Rewards patience, discipline, and consistency

Who & When It Is Best For

Best for:

- Families building long-term wealth
- Parents and grandparents planning inheritance
- Business owners needing liquidity
- Anyone who wants **financial control, stability, and legacy**

Encouragement

Whole Life is **not just insurance**.

It is:

- A **gift**
- A **strategy**
- A **long-range vision**
- A **wealth transfer system**

It says:

"My life matters — and my legacy will continue."

Chapter 11 — Universal Life Insurance (UL)

Flexible Lifetime Protection That Adapts as Life Changes

What It Is

Universal Life (UL) is a type of **permanent life insurance** that provides:

- **Lifetime coverage**
- **Cash value growth**
- And most importantly: **Flexible premiums** and **adjustable death benefit**

This policy is built for people whose life, income, and circumstances may **change**, and they want an insurance policy that can **change with them.**

How It Works

Each premium payment is split into:

Portion	Purpose
Cost of Insurance	Keeps the policy active
Cash Value Account	Accumulates money at interest

The **cash value earns interest**, often tied to **current interest rates**.

If cash value grows well, you may even **lower or skip premium payments** later in life — the policy can **pay itself** temporarily using its own cash value.

You can also **adjust the death benefit** up or down, as your responsibilities change.

What It Is Used For

- Lifelong family protection
- Long-term financial flexibility
- Wealth-building with access to funds when needed

- People whose income may rise and fall
- Protecting legacy during retirement years

UL is the **middle ground** between:

- Term Life (cheap, temporary, no cash value)
  and
- Whole Life (stable, guaranteed growth, higher cost)

Cost

- Higher than Term Life
- Lower than Whole Life (in most cases)
- Price depends on:
  - Age
  - Health
  - Funding level
  - Cash value performance

If managed correctly, UL offers **affordable lifetime protection.**

Pros

Strength	Impact
Flexible Payments	Pay more when income is strong, less when it tightens
Adjustable Coverage	Increase or decrease death benefit over time
Cash Value Access	Borrow or withdraw funds for major milestones
Lifetime Protection	Policy remains active as long as cash value exists

Cons

Limitation	Impact
Requires Monitoring	If underfunded, policy can lapse later
Interest Rate Dependent	Growth may slow in low-rate environments
Not Fully Guaranteed Like Whole Life	Some uncertainty in long-term cash performance

Who & When It's Best For

Best for:

- Business owners
- People with income that fluctuates
- Individuals who value **control and flexibility**
- Families who want **lifetime protection** but lower cost than Whole Life

Encouragement

This policy is for those who say:

"My life may shift — but my protection must remain."

It is **grace + flexibility + legacy** in one package.

Chapter 12 — Indexed Universal Life (IUL)

Market-Linked Growth Without Market Loss — The Wealth Acceleration Policy

What It Is

Indexed Universal Life (IUL) is a **permanent life insurance policy** that provides:

- **Lifetime coverage**
- **Flexible premiums**
- **Cash value growth tied to a market index (like the S&P 500)**
  without exposing you to market downsides.

Meaning:

If the market rises → Your cash value can grow
If the market falls → You **do not lose money**

This is **protected growth**, not speculation.

How It Works

Your cash value growth is determined by:

Mechanism	Meaning
Floor	Minimum credit rate (often 0%–1%), so you **don't lose value**
Cap or Participation Rate	Maximum credited growth or percentage of market growth you receive

So your cash value:

- **Rises when the market rises**
- **Stays safe when the market falls**

Meanwhile:

- You can take **tax-free loans** against the cash value
- While your money **continues earning** inside the policy

This is how families **become their own bank.**

What It Is Used For

- Retirement income *without taxes*
- College funding
- Business capital
- Paying off debt
- Wealth transfer for heirs
- Generational legacy funding

IUL is a **retirement strategy disguised as insurance.**

Cost

- Typically, more expensive than UL
- Less expensive than Whole Life
- Requires consistent funding to unlock full benefits

Pros

Strength	Impact
Market Growth Potential	Grow wealth faster than Whole Life
No Market Loss Risk	Cash value protected from downturns
Tax-Free Loans	Access wealth without tax penalties
Flexible Payments	Adjustable contributions and benefits
Powerful Legacy Tool	Builds inheritance and living benefits

Cons

Limitation	Impact
Must Be Properly Structured	Poor setup can underperform
Requires Consistent Funding	Works best when funded intentionally
Caps Limit Max Growth	Gains are controlled to reduce risk

Who & When It's Best For

Best for:

- People building legacy and long-term wealth
- Business owners and entrepreneurs
- Individuals who want **financial independence without market stress**
- Anyone wanting **tax-free retirement income**

Encouragement

This policy says:

"I will grow wealth without gambling it."

It is **wisdom-based financial strategy.**

Chapter 13 — Variable Universal Life (VUL)

High Growth Potential — High Risk — Investment + Insurance Combined

What It Is

Variable Universal Life (VUL) is a **permanent insurance policy** with:

- Lifetime coverage
- Flexible premiums
- Cash value invested directly in **market sub-accounts** (like mutual funds)

You can earn **high returns**, but you can also **lose value**.

There is **no floor**, no guaranteed growth.

How It Works

Your cash value performance depends on:

- Stock market performance
- Your investment allocation choices
- Market timing decisions

This policy requires **active monitoring** and **investment confidence**.

What It Is Used For

- Aggressive wealth building
- Individuals already familiar with investing
- High-income earners minimizing taxes

This policy is not for beginners — it is for **strategic wealth players.**

Cost

- Higher than Term
- Comparable to IUL or UL
- Policy returns vary significantly — some years strong, some years negative

Pros

Strength	Impact
Highest Growth Potential	Can outperform all other life insurance types
Full Investment Control	You choose the funds and allocations
Tax-Deferred Growth	Gains grow without immediate taxation
Tax-Free Loans Possible	If managed correctly, can pull income without taxes

Cons

Limitation	Impact
Risk of Significant Loss	Market downturns can reduce cash value
Requires Financial Discipline	Not suitable for hands-off owners
Higher Fees	Investment management + insurance fees combined
Policy Can Lapse	If cash value drops too low, premiums can spike

Who & When It's Best For

Best for:

- Investors comfortable with market volatility
- High-income earners needing tax-advantaged growth
- People who already have financial stability and discipline

Not Recommended for:

- Financial beginners
- Unstable income situations
- People who fear market swings

Encouragement

This policy says:

"I am a builder who understands both faith and strategy."

It is a tool for **those prepared to manage it wisely and intentionally.**

Chapter 14 — Guaranteed Universal Life (GUL)

Lifetime Protection at Lower Cost — Security Without the Complexity

What It Is

Guaranteed Universal Life (GUL) is a **permanent life insurance policy** designed to provide **lifetime coverage** at a **lower cost**, by focusing on **guaranteeing the death benefit** rather than building large cash value.

This is sometimes described as:

"Whole Life protection at Term Life pricing."

It protects your family **for life**, but does **not focus on wealth-building** like Whole Life or IUL.

How It Works

- You select an age to guarantee coverage to (90, 95, 100, 105, 110, or 121).
- You pay a **fixed premium** that does **not change**.
- As long as payments are made, the **death benefit is guaranteed**, regardless of:
    - Health changes
    - Market changes
    - Economy shifts

Cash value is **minimal** — the focus is **pure lifelong protection**.

What It Is Used For

- Ensuring your family **never loses your coverage**
- Leaving a **guaranteed inheritance**
- Covering **final expenses**, debt payoff, or legacy gifts
- Estate planning with predictable cost
- Providing **financial peace** for spouses and children

Cost

- **More expensive than Term**
- **Less expensive than Whole Life or IUL**
- Cost is based on:
    - Age
    - Health
    - Coverage amount
    - Guarantee length (to age 100 costs more than to age 90)

This is a **value-focused permanent policy.**

Pros

Strength	Impact
Lifetime Coverage	Protection never expires
Fixed Premium	Cost stays the same permanently
Lower Cost Than Most Permanent Insurance	Makes lifelong coverage accessible

Strength	Impact
Simple + Low-Maintenance	No investing, monitoring, or fund decisions

Cons

Limitation	Impact
Little to No Cash Value	Not a wealth-building tool
No Market Growth Opportunity	No retirement income benefits
Not Designed for Loans/Withdrawals	Best used strictly for protection

Who & When It's Best For

Best for:

- Seniors who want **affordable lifetime peace of mind**

- Families who want **guaranteed inheritance** without cash accumulation
- People who waited too long to buy Whole Life
- Anyone who says:
  "I just want to make sure my family is protected, no matter what."

Encouragement

This policy says:

"I will not leave financial chaos when God calls me home."

It is **love, dignity, and preparation expressed with wisdom.**

Chapter 15 — Survivorship / Second-to-Die Life Insurance

The Legacy Policy That Protects Generations — Not Just a Household

What It Is

Survivorship Life Insurance (also called **Second-to-Die Insurance**) is a single life insurance policy that covers **two people**, usually **a married couple**, and **pays out only after both have passed.**

This policy is **not about income replacement.** It is about **generational inheritance and estate protection.**

How It Works

- Two people are insured under one policy.

- No benefit is paid when the **first person** passes.
- The **full tax-free benefit** is paid **after the second person passes.**

This payout is strategically timed when **the family needs it most** — during **wealth transfer**.

What It Is Used For

- **Passing wealth to children and grandchildren**
- Protecting inheritance from **tax erosion**
- Funding **trusts, endowments, scholarships**
- Keeping **family businesses** in the family
- Equalizing inheritance when assets are not easily divided

This is **legacy insurance**, not survival insurance.

Cost

- **Less expensive** than buying two separate permanent policies
- Pricing is favorable because the payout is delayed until both insured lives end

This makes legacy planning **more affordable**.

Pros

Strength	Impact
High Legacy Value	Directly strengthens generational financial foundation
Cost-Efficient	Two lives covered for less cost
Estate Tax Strategy	Protects inheritance from being consumed by taxes
Perfect for Trust Planning	Works beautifully with wills and estate structures

Cons

Limitation	Impact
No Payout After First Death	Not designed for income replacement

Limitation	Impact
Requires Estate Planning Knowledge	Works best when combined with trust or legal structure
Family Must Be Organized	Must have beneficiary and inheritance plan documented

Who & When It's Best For

Best for:

- Married couples building wealth together
- Families with real estate, businesses, or investment assets
- Parents and grandparents serious about **legacy**
- People who want to make sure future generations are protected

Encouragement

This policy says:

"Our love and our work will outlive us."

This is **Proverbs 13:22 stewardship in action.**

Chapter 16 – Single Premium Life Insurance

One Payment. Lifetime Coverage. Instant Inheritance.

What It Is

Single Premium Life Insurance is a permanent life policy that is **paid in full upfront** with **one lump-sum payment**.

No monthly bills.
No ongoing payment schedule.
Coverage is **locked in for life** immediately.

How It Works

- You pay once (example: $10k, $25k, $50k, $100k+).
- The policy immediately provides a **larger death benefit**.

- The policy begins to accumulate **cash value**, which can grow and be borrowed if needed.

This is **immediate legacy multiplication.**

Example:

$25,000 deposit → $60,000–$90,000 tax-free inheritance.

Your one seed becomes **many seeds**.

What It Is Used For

- Guaranteeing children or grandchildren receive inheritance
- Turning savings into **legacy**
- Replacing taxable bank accounts with **tax-free transfer**
- Protecting assets from probate delays
- Creating instant family blessing

Cost

- Cost depends on the **one-time deposit amount**
- There are **no ongoing premiums**
- Works best for people with:
    - Savings
    - Retirement funds
    - Settlement payouts
    - CD or money market accounts earning low interest

Pros

Strength	Impact
One Payment — Done Forever	No future financial obligation
Immediate Legacy Leverage	Your deposit multiplies instantly
Cash Value Growth	Wealth grows tax-deferred
Tax-Free Transfer to Heirs	Keeps wealth intact

Cons

Limitation	Impact
Requires Lump Sum	Not everyone has capital available upfront
Not Designed for Monthly Budget Buyers	Best for savers, retirees, and investors

Who & When It's Best For

Best for:

- Retirees with savings or CDs
- Parents/grandparents who want to **leave something meaningful**
- Individuals who want to **turn savings into legacy**
- People who want inheritance to transfer **quickly and privately**

Encouragement

This policy says:

"I will not just leave memories — I will leave provision."

This is legacy delivered with **dignity, honor, and purpose.**

Chapter 17 — Child / Juvenile Whole Life Insurance

Planting Financial Roots So Strong That No Storm in Adulthood Can Uproot Them

What It Is

Child or Juvenile Whole Life Insurance is a **permanent life insurance policy** purchased for a **child** (usually by a parent or grandparent). It guarantees:

- **Lifetime coverage**
- **Locked-in premium rates that never increase**
- **Cash value that grows every year, guaranteed**
- The right to **purchase more coverage later** — even if their health changes

This policy is not just insurance.
It is **financial foundation.**
It is **identity reinforcement.**
It is **legacy preparation.**

It tells the child:

"We believe in your future enough to prepare for it today."

How It Works

You choose a coverage amount (example: $25,000, $50,000, $100,000).
You pay a **small monthly premium** — often **$10–$40** depending on age and coverage.

Each payment does three things:

1. **Keeps the policy active for life**
2. **Builds cash value that grows automatically**
3. **Locks in insurability forever**

The **younger** the child is when the policy is purchased:

- The **lower** the premium
- The **faster** the cash value grows
- The **stronger** the long-term financial benefit becomes

When the child turns 18 or 21, ownership can be transferred to them —
or you can keep ownership for long-term guidance.

What It Is Used For

- Ensuring the child **always has life insurance**, no matter what happens later
- Establishing **cash reserves** that can be used for:
    - First car
    - College expenses
    - Starting a business
    - Buying a home
    - Paying off debt
    - Wedding costs
    - Emergency funds

    - Retirement income later in life
- Teaching **financial responsibility from childhood**
- Creating generational legacy **on purpose**

This is how we **break generational money anxiety**.
By planting structure **before the struggle ever begins.**

Cost

Child Whole Life is one of the **most affordable** forms of insurance.

Example premiums:

Child Age	$25K Policy	$50K Policy
Newborn	$12–$18/mo	$22–$35/mo
Age 5	$14–$22/mo	$26–$40/mo
Age 10	$18–$28/mo	$32–$48/mo

The premium is **locked in for life**.

If the child develops:

- Asthma
- Diabetes
- Autism
- Epilepsy
- Mental health disorders
- Heart issues
- Cancer
- Disability

Their **insurance cannot be taken away or changed.**

This is **protection from the unknown future.**

Pros

Strength	Impact
Lifetime Coverage	The child will never be uninsured
Low, Locked-In Premiums	Rates never increase — even in adulthood
Builds Cash Value	Creates usable wealth that grows tax-deferred
Guaranteed Insurability	Illness or disabilities later cannot cancel coverage

Strength	Impact
Wealth Education Tool	A practical entry to teaching stewardship

Cons

Limitation	Impact
Cash Value Grows Slowly Early	True value appears over decades, not months
Not Designed for Quick Cash Accumulation	Works best when held long-term
Requires Commitment and Consistency	Works for families focused on long-term legacy

Who & When It's Best For

Best for:

- Parents who want to give their child a **financial head start**
- Grandparents who want to leave **living legacy**

- Families committed to **breaking generational financial struggle**
- Households who understand that **wealth is built early, slowly, and intentionally**

Best Time to Start:
The **day the child is born** — or as early as possible.

Time is the greatest multiplier in this policy.

Why This Policy Changes Generations

This policy **transfers more than money.**

It transfers:

- **Security**
- **Confidence**
- **Identity**
- **Preparedness**
- **Financial maturity**
- **Legacy wisdom**

The child grows up **knowing**:

- "My family planned for me."
- "I come from people who think ahead."
- "I am valuable."

That is identity wealth.
And identity wealth is the **root of financial wealth.**

Encouragement

This policy is a **seed.**
A seed that grows roots before the wind shows up.
A seed that becomes a shelter when life gets rough.
A seed that says:

"You will not start where we started — you will start where we finished."

This is generational love.
This is generational leadership.
This is generational strategy.

This is **legacy on purpose.**

Chapter 18 — Final Expense / Burial Insurance

Removing Financial Burden from Your Family During Their Most Vulnerable Moment

What It Is

Final Expense Insurance (also called **Burial Insurance** or **End-of-Life Insurance**) is a **small permanent life insurance policy** designed to cover:

- Funeral and memorial costs
- Burial or cremation expenses
- Medical bills
- Final household bills
- Outstanding debts

Its purpose is simple:

To prevent your loved ones from having to raise money, borrow, or struggle to bury you.

This policy is one of the **purest forms of love and dignity.**

How It Works

- You choose a **coverage amount** (typically $5,000 to $50,000).
- You pay a **fixed monthly premium** that **never increases.**
- The **death benefit never decreases.**
- The policy **never expires**, as long as premiums are paid.
- When you transition, your family receives the **full tax-free benefit**.

This allows them to:

- Grieve in peace
- Honor your life respectfully
- Avoid unnecessary financial stress

No scrambling.
No fundraising.
No embarrassment.
Just dignity.

What It Is Used For

- Funeral home services
- Casket or cremation costs
- Burial plot and headstone
- Flowers, transportation, and repast
- Small lingering medical or credit bills
- Transition support for spouse or children

It **replaces panic with peace** at a moment when they will need peace the most.

Cost

Final Expense is designed to be **affordable**, especially for seniors or people on fixed income.

Premiums are based on:

- Age
- Health status
- Tobacco or non-tobacco use
- Coverage amount

Typical premium ranges:

Age	$10,000 Coverage	$20,000 Coverage
50	$25–$45/mo	$45–$85/mo
60	$35–$65/mo	$70–$125/mo
70	$55–$95/mo	$110–$185/mo

The older you wait → the more expensive it becomes.
So the best time is always now.

Pros

Strength	Impact
Easy Approval	Even with health conditions, many are approved
No Medical Exam	Most policies use simple health questions

Strength	Impact
Premium Never Increases	Fixed cost brings long-term peace of mind
Coverage Never Decreases	Your family receives the full amount
Policy Never Expires	Lasts for life, not just for a term

This is **security that does not break.**

Cons

Limitation	Impact
Smaller Coverage Amounts	Not designed to replace income or build wealth
More Expensive Than Term (Per Dollar)	But easier to obtain for seniors
Cash Value Grows Slowly	Wealth building is not the priority here

This is **not a legacy policy** — this is a **protection-of-dignity policy.**

Who & When It's Best For

Best for:

- Seniors
- People on fixed income (Social Security, SSI, Disability)
- Individuals with medical conditions who cannot qualify for other life insurance
- Adults who do not want to leave loved ones with funeral debt
- Children of aging parents who want to prevent financial hardship later

Best Time to Get It:
Before health changes.
Before senior premiums rise.
Before the burden falls on your children.

Why This Matters Emotionally

Without Final Expense Insurance, families often face:

- $8,000–$15,000 in funeral costs **immediately**
- Decision-making under stress and grief
- The pressure of:
    - Car washes
    - Church donations
    - GoFundMe campaigns
    - Loans
    - Embarrassment
    - Shame

But with this policy:

- The funeral is already paid for.
- The family is not financially disrupted.
- The memorial can be **beautiful, honorable, and peaceful**.

This policy protects **the emotional well-being** of the family — not just the financial.

Encouragement

This policy says:

"My family will not struggle because of my passing."

It is compassion in advance.
It is protection that speaks when you no longer can.
It is **love expressed through preparation.**

When we truly love our family — we don't just love them while we are here,
we **love them in how we leave.**

Chapter 19 — Credit Life Insurance

Protecting the Debt, Not the Family — And Why That Distinction Matters

What It Is

Credit Life Insurance is a type of insurance designed to **pay off a specific loan** if the borrower dies before the loan is repaid.

This could be:

- A **car loan**
- A **credit card**
- A **personal loan**
- A **furniture or store financing loan**
- In some cases, even a **small mortgage**

However, the key point is this:

The lender — not the family — receives the insurance payout.

This insurance **protects the bank**, not the household.

How It Works

When you take out a loan, the lender may offer (or strongly suggest) Credit Life Insurance.

You pay a **premium**, either:

- Added to your monthly loan payment, or
- Included up front in the loan amount

If you die before the loan is paid:

- The **remaining balance is paid directly to the lender**

Your family **does not receive** any cash benefit. They receive only the **paid-off loan**.

This prevents them from inheriting debt —
but it **does not build legacy or leave income.**

What It Is Used For

- Ensuring a spouse or co-signer doesn't inherit loan payments
- Protecting a family from losing property tied to a loan
- Covering debts for someone who **cannot qualify** for traditional life insurance

This policy exists to prevent **financial burden**, not to build wealth.

Cost

Credit Life Insurance is often:

- **More expensive than Term Life Insurance**
- Automatically added to loan paperwork without clear explanation
- Based on loan amount — not age or health

This means many people pay **more than necessary** for protection that **benefits the lender, not the family.**

Pros

Strength	Impact
No Medical Exam	Easy approval, even with health issues
Debt Doesn't Fall on Family	Protects co-signers and surviving spouse
Simple & Automatic	Often added directly to loan payments

This is **convenience insurance**, not strategic insurance.

Cons

Limitation	Impact
Lender Gets the Money	Family receives **no inheritance**
Coverage Declines Over Time	Benefit shrinks as loan balance decreases

Limitation	Impact
Premium Usually Stays the Same	Paying the same amount for **less coverage each year**
Often More Expensive Than Term Life	You pay extra for convenience, not value

What starts out sounding helpful can quickly become **a poor stewardship move**.

Who & When It's Best For

Best for:

- Someone who **cannot medically qualify** for any other life insurance
- Individuals with **serious health conditions**
- People who simply want to ensure **no debt is passed on**

Not Ideal for:

- People who are healthy enough to qualify for:
  - **Term Life**
  - **Whole Life**
  - **IUL**
  - **GUL**
  - etc.

Because those policies:

- Cost less
- Offer higher value
- Protect **the family**, not the lender

Your Teaching Insight

Credit Life Insurance answers the question:

- *"How do I prevent debt from becoming a burden?"*

But it does **not** answer the question:

- *"How do I create legacy and generational security?"*

If someone is financially rebuilding, this policy can be a **temporary defense**,
but it should **not** be the long-term strategy.

Better Strategy (If Health Allows)

Use:

- **Level Term Insurance** or
- **Whole Life**
  or
- **IUL**

Instead of Credit Life.

With Term or Whole Life:

- Your **family receives the money**
- They can **choose** whether to pay the loan off
- They keep the **surplus** as **inheritance**

This is the difference between:

- **Protecting a loan**
  and
- **Protecting a legacy.**

Encouragement

This chapter is **not about shame.**
It is about **awareness.**

Because once we **see clearly**, we can **choose wisely.**

This chapter empowers us to say:

"I will no longer make financial decisions that only benefit the lender.
I will make decisions that bless my family, my lineage, and my legacy."

This is how we break the cycle of:

- Borrow → Pay → Owe → Leave Nothing

And step into:

- Plan → Protect → Build → Leave Inheritance

This is **financial leadership.**
This is **spiritual maturity.**
This is **legacy alignment.**

Chapter 20 — Group Life Insurance

A Good Start — But Not a Complete Strategy

What It Is

Group Life Insurance is life insurance that is provided through an organization — most commonly your **employer**, union, fraternity, church staff plan, or professional association.

It is typically offered in two parts:

1. **Basic Group Life**
   - Automatically included
   - Often equal to **one year of your salary**
2. **Supplemental Group Life**
   - Optional extra coverage
   - You may pay a low monthly premium for increased protection

This type of insurance is designed to make sure **everyone has at least some coverage** — even if their finances or health are not perfect.

How It Works

- The employer negotiates the insurance contract.
- The company either **pays all**, or shares the cost with the employee.
- As long as you are **actively employed**, your coverage remains active.
- If you **leave your job**, the coverage usually **ends immediately**.

This policy is **tied to the job, not the family.**

What It Is Used For

- Providing **basic protection** at a low cost
- Offering coverage to those who **may not qualify elsewhere**
- Supplementing insurance during working years

- Acting as **starter protection** while building a full plan

This policy ensures your family is **not completely unprotected** — but it is **not enough by itself.**

Cost

One of the reasons Group Life is popular is because it is **affordable.**

Cost benefits include:

- **Employer may pay some or all of the premium**
- **Supplemental coverage** is usually cheaper than private coverage
- **No medical exam** or health qualification required for basic coverage

This makes Group Life a **great entry point** — but not a final solution.

Pros

Strength	Impact
Low or No Cost	Makes protection accessible to everyone
Easy to Qualify	Little to no health requirements
Immediate Coverage	Protection begins quickly after employment
Convenient Payroll Deductions	No billing headaches

Group Life is **grace** — it fills the gap when life is unstable.

Cons

Limitation	Impact
Coverage Ends When the Job Ends	If you quit, retire, or are laid off — your family loses protection

Limitation	Impact
Not Enough Coverage	One year's salary is rarely enough to protect a family
No Cash Value	Cannot borrow from it or build wealth with it
No Control	The employer controls the policy — not you

This is why **depending on Group Life alone puts families at risk.**

Who & When It's Best For

Best for:

- Individuals just starting their financial journey
- People who currently cannot afford their own policy yet
- Employees who want **supplemental coverage** while building savings
- Anyone with **existing health conditions** who needs coverage access

Not Ideal as:

- A **primary** life insurance plan
- A **legacy building** tool
- Long-term protection into retirement

Because:

When your employment ends — the coverage ends.
But your family's need does **not** end.

Your Teaching Insight

Group Life Insurance is:

- **Support**, not **foundation**
- **Assistance**, not **strategy**
- **A cushion**, not **a legacy plan**

It fills the **gap**, but it does **not** build the **future**.

A family should **never** have to pray you keep your job just so they can keep their financial protection.

Your **personal policy** is your **legacy**.
Group Life is just a **benefit**.

Better Strategy

Use **Group Life as supplemental coverage**, not primary.

Your personal plan should be built from:

- **Term Life Insurance (for income protection)**
- **Whole Life or IUL (for wealth and legacy)**

Your **job should not own your family's financial security**.

Encouragement

This policy is a **start**, not a finish line.

It is **training wheels** — not the full bicycle.

It says:

"I am covering my family with what I have today — but I am also preparing to cover them with what I am building tomorrow."

This is **progress.**
This is **responsibility.**
This is **financial growth in motion.**

Chapter 21 — Mortgage Life Insurance

Protecting the House Without Protecting the Legacy — Understanding the Difference

What It Is

Mortgage Life Insurance is a policy designed specifically to **pay off your mortgage** if you pass away before the loan is paid in full.

But here is the key that most people miss:

The beneficiary is the bank — not your family.

Meaning:

- The mortgage balance will be eliminated
- But **your loved ones will not receive any money**

The home is protected, but **legacy is not created.**

How It Works

- You take out a mortgage (ex. $280,000).
- The mortgage company or lender **offers** Mortgage Life Insurance.
- If you pass away during the mortgage term:
    - The remaining mortgage balance is **paid directly to the lender**.
    - Your spouse or children **inherit the house**, mortgage-free.

Coverage **decreases** as the mortgage balance decreases.
But your **premium usually stays the same**.

So over time:

- You pay the **same amount of money**
- For **less and less protection**

What It Is Used For

- Preventing the family from losing the home
- Ensuring **housing stability** during grief
- Protecting a spouse who cannot afford payments alone
- Protecting co-signers from financial hardship

This policy prevents **loss**, but does **not create future security.**

Cost

Mortgage Life Insurance is often:

- **More expensive** than Term Life
- **Less flexible**
- **Harder to transfer to another home**
- And sometimes **bundled into your mortgage without clear explanation**

You're paying for **convenience**, not strategy.

Pros

Strength	Impact
Ensures the Home Is Paid Off	Family doesn't lose the house
Easy Approval	Often **no medical exam** required
Immediate Coverage	Usually begins at closing
Protects Co-Signers	Prevents inherited debt

For households with fragile or limited health options, this policy can be a **life-saver**.

Cons

Limitation	Impact
Bank Gets the Money — Not the Family	No financial flexibility or inheritance
Coverage Declines Each Year	Benefit shrinks as mortgage shrinks

Limitation	Impact
Premium Usually Stays the Same	Paying full price for shrinking benefit
Not Transferable	If you refinance or move, you may lose the policy
No Cash Value	Cannot borrow from or grow wealth

This is **protection**, not **legacy**.

Who & When It's Best For

Best for:

- Someone who **cannot medically qualify** for Term Life Insurance
- People with **health issues** or limited insurability
- Individuals who simply want to **guarantee the home stays in the family**

- Seniors refinancing or taking late-life mortgages

Not Ideal for:

- Those who are **healthy enough** to qualify for:
    - **Level Term**
    - **Whole Life**
    - **IUL**
    - **GUL**

Why?

Because those policies:

- Cost less (in most cases)
- Pay **your family**, not the bank
- Provide **flexibility**
- Leave **inheritance**, not just relief

The Better Strategy (When Health Allows)

Replace Mortgage Life Insurance with a Level Term Policy.

Example:

Instead of buying:

- $250,000 Mortgage Life Insurance

Buy:

- **$250,000 Level Term Life Insurance** (same or lower cost)

If you pass:

- Your family receives **$250,000 in cash**
- They **choose** whether to pay the mortgage
- **Any leftover becomes inheritance**

This shifts:

- **Control**
- **Power**
- **Choice**

Back to **your family**, where it belongs.

Author's Insight

Mortgage Life Insurance answers the question:

"How do we keep the house?"

But wise financial planning asks:

"How do we protect the house AND the family?"

One prevents loss.
The other **creates legacy.**

Encouragement

This chapter is not about guilt —
it is about **awakening**.

It is the moment where we say:

"I will not just keep my family from losing the house —
I will empower them to live after I am gone."

This is where protection becomes **provision**.
Provision becomes **legacy**.
Legacy becomes **inheritance.**

And inheritance becomes **love that continues speaking even after your voice is silent.**

Chapter 22 – Key Person Insurance

Protecting the Vision, the Leadership, and the Mission God Assigned to Your Organization

What It Is

Key Person Insurance is a life insurance policy that a **business, ministry, nonprofit, or organization** takes out on a leader whose **presence is essential** to the success, direction, revenue, stability, and future of the organization.

This could be:

- A founder
- A senior pastor
- A business owner
- A top-producing salesperson
- A CFO or finance director

- A leader whose influence cannot be easily replaced

The **organization**:

- **Owns** the policy
- **Pays** the premiums
- **Receives** the death benefit

It is designed to protect the **mission**, the **people**, and the **work** if that leader transitions unexpectedly.

How It Works

1. The organization identifies a key individual whose role is critical.
2. The organization purchases a **life insurance policy** on that person.
3. The organization pays the monthly or annual premium.
4. If the key individual passes away:
    - The **organization** receives the payout — **not the family**.

The funds are used to:

- Maintain payroll
- Keep operations running
- Pay down debts or financial commitments
- Hire and train a replacement
- Provide stability during transition
- Reassure donors, members, board members, investors, and staff

This policy **protects the assignment** from collapse.

What It Is Used For

- Ensuring the business or ministry does not shut down after a leadership loss
- Preventing financial crisis during transition
- Preserving the integrity and continuity of the vision
- Securing staff, members, and clients from instability
- Funding leadership search, training, and onboarding

This is **organizational stewardship**.

This is leadership that says:

"The calling must continue, even if the leader no longer can."

Cost

Cost is determined by:

- Age and health of the key leader
- Amount of coverage needed
- The financial value of the leader to the organization

Typical coverage amounts:

- $100,000 for small organizations
- $250,000–$1,000,000 for mid-size
- $1,000,000–$10,000,000+ for large companies

Premiums are paid by the organization, not the individual.

This is a **business expense**, and in many cases, may be **tax-deductible** depending on structure and usage.

Pros

Strength	Impact
Protects the Organization's Stability	Prevents collapse during leadership loss
Funds Replacement and Transition	Allows for intentional leadership succession
Reassures Staff, Customers & Donors	Provides stability during uncertainty
Maintains Payroll & Operations	Ensures employees are not harmed financially
Supports Strategic Continuity	Keeps the mission moving forward

This is how organizations **survive shock and maintain vision.**

Cons

Limitation	Impact
Does Not Replace the Leader Themselves	Leadership development must still be intentional
Must Be Strategically Planned	Requires clear roles and valuation of leadership
Does Not Provide Family Inheritance	Family needs separate personal insurance

This policy protects the **organization**, not the household.

Both the family and the organization need **their own coverage**.

Who & When It's Best For

Best for:

- Churches (Senior Pastor & Executive Leadership)

- Nonprofits with strong community leadership presence
- Family-owned businesses
- Partnerships and entrepreneurial teams
- Real estate brokerages, law firms, medical practices, consulting firms
- Any organization that depends on **one key person**

Critical Situations:

- When one person carries most of the relationships
- When one person carries most of the income production
- When one person carries the vision or direction

If losing that person would:

- Slow down operations
- Damage stability
- Stop expansion
- Reduce giving, sales, or revenue
- Create confusion

Then **Key Person Insurance is mandatory stewardship.**

Your Teaching Insight

This policy is not just financial.

It is spiritual.

It recognizes:

- **Leadership is a calling**
- **Assignments are larger than individuals**
- **The work must continue even after we transition**

This is leadership maturity.

This is legacy leadership.

This is saying:

"The mission will not die when I do."

Encouragement

This chapter is the moment an organization steps into **wisdom over assumption**.

Instead of hoping things will work out, you **prepare**.

Instead of reacting to crisis, you **protect the mission before crisis arrives**.

This is **strategy.**
This is **structure.**
This is **legacy-level stewardship.**

Key Person Insurance speaks loudly:

"God's work through us will continue beyond us."

And that, is how **visions outlive the visionary**.

Chapter 23 — Buy-Sell Agreement Insurance

Protecting Partnership, Preventing Conflict, and Preserving the Vision

What It Is

A **Buy-Sell Agreement** is a legally binding contract between business partners that says:

If one partner dies (or becomes disabled), the remaining partner(s) will buy out their share of the business.

Buy-Sell Agreement Insurance provides the **money needed** to make that buyout possible — **quickly and peacefully.**

The **business or the surviving partner(s)** receive the insurance payout and use it to **purchase the ownership interest** of the deceased partner from their family.

This protects:

- The **business**
- The **partnership**
- The **vision**
- And the **family of the deceased**

Why This Matters

When a partner passes away:

- Their ownership share **automatically transfers to their spouse or heirs**
- But the spouse may **not know the business**
- The surviving partner may **not have the funds to buy them out**
- Which can cause:
    - Disagreements
    - Legal disputes
    - Financial strain
    - Forced business sale
    - Business collapse

A Buy-Sell Agreement with insurance prevents **all of this**.

It keeps **peace**, **structure**, and **stability**.

How It Works

1. A Buy-Sell Agreement is drafted by an attorney.
2. Each partner is insured with a **life insurance policy**.
3. The **business** or the partners **own** the policy and pay the premiums.
4. If one partner passes:
    - The surviving partner(s) or business receives the **insurance payout**
    - Those funds are used to **buy** the deceased partner's ownership share
    - The family receives **fair financial value**, not business responsibility
    - The surviving partner retains **full control and continuity**

This is how **legacy stays organized**.

What It Is Used For

- Ensuring the surviving partner **keeps control** of the business
- Ensuring the deceased partner's family receives **fair compensation**
- Preventing **conflict** and **confusion**
- Protecting:
    - Brand
    - Staff
    - Clients
    - Revenue
    - Vision continuity

This is **responsible partnership**.

Cost

Cost varies based on:

- Partner ages
- Health status

- Coverage amount (equal to partner equity value)

Example:
If each partner owns **50% of a $600,000 company**, each needs a policy of **$300,000**.

Premiums are usually **tax-deductible business expenses**, depending on structure.

This is **one of the most valuable and affordable business protections available.**

Pros

Strength	Impact
Prevents Legal and Family Conflict	No disputes, no guessing, no pressure
Ensures Business Continuity	Keeps the company operating smoothly
Guarantees Fair Compensation to Family	Heirs receive value, not stress
Protects Vision and Leadership	No forced sale or takeover

Strength	Impact
Strengthens Partnership Trust	Everyone knows the plan is secure

This is **relationship protection + business protection.**

Cons

Limitation	Impact
Requires Legal Structuring	Needs an attorney to draft correctly
Requires Accurate Valuation	Business value must be reviewed regularly
Premiums Must Be Maintained	Policies must stay active for protection to work

But these are **minor responsibilities** compared to the **disasters this policy prevents.**

Who & When It's Best For

Best for:

- Business partners
- Small to mid-size privately owned companies
- Family-owned businesses
- LLCs, S-corps, and partnerships
- Churches or ministries co-led by multiple leaders
- Real estate investment groups
- Medical, law, consulting, accounting firms

Mandatory When:

- Two or more people own a business together
- Family inheritance expectations exist
- The business would suffer financially if one partner dies

Your Teaching Insight

This policy protects:

- **Legacy**

- **Relationship**
- **Stability**
- **Vision**

It ensures that:

- The family is honored
- The business is preserved
- The partnership is respected
- The transition is peaceful

This policy prevents **the enemy's favorite tactics**:

- Confusion
- Conflict
- Division

It keeps unity intact.

Encouragement

This agreement says:

"Our partnership is bigger than one lifetime."

It is:

- Wisdom.
- Stewardship.
- Love.
- Structure.
- Legacy planning.
- Honor in action.

It ensures the **business does not die when a person does**.
It ensures the **family receives blessing, not burden.**
It ensures the **vision remains alive, advancing, and fruitful.**

This is how you **build something that outlives you.**

Section Three: Stages for Insurance

Chapter 24 — Childhood (Ages 0–18)

This Is the Planting Stage — The Financial Roots of Identity and Legacy

Mindset of This Stage

A child is not earning income.
A child is not supporting a household.
So we do **not** insure a child for **income replacement.**

We insure them for:

- **Guaranteed insurability**
- **Financial head start**
- **Slow, steady wealth foundation**
- **Identity shaping and legacy grounding**

This is **roots, not leaves.**

Best Policy for This Stage

Child / Juvenile Whole Life Insurance

Why

- Low premiums that **never increase**
- Cash value that **grows every year**
- Locks in insurability **before life happens**
- Sets a foundation of **ownership, planning, and dignity**

Financial Benefit

- Can be transferred to the child in adulthood
- Can be borrowed from later for:
    - College
    - First home
    - Wedding
    - Business startup
    - Emergency support

Legacy Purpose

This policy says:

"You will not start where we started. You will start where we left off."

Child life insurance is not about **death** —
it is about **positioning their life to begin ahead of struggle.**

Chapter 25 — Young Life (Ages 18–25)

This Is the Identity and Launch Stage — Protect the Future, Not the Moment

Mindset of This Stage

This is when individuals:

- Begin working
- May begin college or trade school
- Begin building independence
- Often **don't think about risk**
- Believe they have "all the time in the world"

This is the stage where **habits shape destiny**.

Best Policy for This Stage

Convertible Level Term Insurance + Keep the Childhood Whole Life Policy

Why

- They now have income to protect — even if small
- They are building credit and may accumulate debt
- They may start families unexpectedly
- They need **low-cost protection with room to grow**

The **Convertible Term** allows them to:

- Start with minimal cost
- Upgrade later to Whole Life or IUL
- Without needing to medically qualify again

Cost Advantage

This stage has **the cheapest premiums of their life**.

Locking in rates now is a **lifelong blessing**.

Legacy Purpose

This policy says:

"I'm beginning adulthood with wisdom, not reaction."

This is where responsibility becomes **identity**, not burden.

Chapter 26 — Early Adulthood (Ages 25–35)

This Is the Expansion Stage — Career, Family, Assets, and Responsibility Rise

Mindset of This Stage

This is when life begins to:

- Move fast
- Get expensive
- Gain emotional and financial responsibility:

Common realities:

- Marriage / partnership
- Children
- Mortgage or renting responsibility
- Career building
- Starting businesses
- Student loans
- Auto loans

This is the **most financially vulnerable stage of adult life**.

Best Policy for This Stage

Large Level Term Policy (20–30 Year) + Begin Wealth Policy (IUL or Whole Life)

Why this combination works

Policy	Purpose
Level Term	Protects the family's survival if income is lost
IUL or Whole Life	Starts building generational wealth and financial stability

Term protects **right now.**
IUL/Whole Life builds **forever.**

Cost Advantage

This stage still qualifies for **low premiums**, so:

- The biggest coverage costs the least here
- Delaying increases cost dramatically

Legacy Purpose

This policy says:

'My family will not go backwards because I am no longer here."

This is where **legacy begins to take structure**, not just intention.

Chapter 27 — Mid-Life (Ages 35–55)

This Is the Legacy Construction Stage — Protect, Build, and Multiply

Mindset of This Stage

This stage often carries the **weight of many roles**:

- Raising children
- Caring for aging parents
- Managing a career or business
- Paying mortgages and debts
- Supporting spouse or community
- Trying to plan for retirement

This is the season where:

- Your **income is highest**
- Your **responsibilities are highest**
- Your **time feels shortest**

This is where **legacy is no longer theory** — it is **daily responsibility.**

The Risk

If death occurs in this stage:

- The family loses the **primary financial engine**
- Children and spouse face immediate lifestyle collapse
- Debts and mortgage may become unmanageable
- Business or ministry may fall apart
- Dreams may die with the dreamer

This stage carries the **highest stakes**.

Best Policy Strategy

Term + Whole Life or IUL (Dual Strategy)

Policy	Role
Term Life Insurance (20–30 years)	Protects income, home, family stability RIGHT NOW
IUL or Whole Life	Builds wealth, cash value, and legacy for the future

Why this works best:

- Term covers your **peak responsibility years**
- Whole Life / IUL builds **long-term generational wealth**

You are **protecting your present** while **funding your future**.

Financial Reasoning

This is the stage where **cash flow is real**.

You have the power to:

- Pay off debt
- Increase investing

- Build retirement
- Purchase properties
- Create trust funds
- Fund business expansion

The IUL or Whole Life policy becomes:

- A **tax-free savings account**
- A **borrowing system**
- A **retirement income tool**
- A **wealth transfer vehicle**

This is how you **stop consuming and begin constructing.**

Legacy Purpose

This stage says:

"My family will not just survive because of me — they will rise because of me."

This is the season where **wealth stops being something you dream about**
and becomes something you **build intentionally.**

Chapter 28 — Seasoned Life (Ages 55–69)

This Is the Preservation and Transfer Stage — Protect What You Built

Mindset of This Stage

At this point:

- Children may be grown
- Retirement is near or already in planning
- Health may begin to shift
- Purpose and meaning become more important than possessions

This is the season of:

- Reflection
- Refinement
- Stewardship

You are asking:

- *What will I leave?*
- *How will I be remembered?*
- *Will my family struggle or be secure?*

The Risk

Waiting too long reduces:

- Coverage qualification
- Affordability
- Financial efficiency

This is the stage where many people say:
"I should have done this sooner."

But **grace is still available.**

Best Policy Strategy

Guaranteed Universal Life (GUL) or Whole Life

- Optional **Single Premium Life** if savings are available

Policy	Role
GUL	Affordable lifetime coverage with no expiration
Whole Life	Legacy + cash value + stable premiums
Single Premium Life	Converts savings into *instant inheritance*

Why this works best:

- You secure **lifetime protection**
- You prevent **funeral & end-of-life stress**
- You create **inheritance instead of burden**
- You **lock in** rates before health declines further

Financial Reasoning

This stage is about **efficiency**, not aggression.

Focus is now on:

- Stability
- Predictability
- Guaranteed outcomes

This is not the season for high-risk financial instruments.

This is the season for **certainty.**

Legacy Purpose

This stage says:

"I have lived well — now I will leave well."

This is **dignity, honor, and foresight** in action.

Chapter 29 — Senior Life (Ages 69+)

This Is the Legacy Fulfillment Stage — Peace, Dignity, and Final Blessing

Mindset of This Stage

This stage brings:

- Wisdom
- Memory
- Completion
- Reflection

Life is no longer about **accumulation** — it is about **closure, love, and meaning**.

The goal is:

- **Peace for your family**
- **Clarity for your affairs**
- **Grace for your departure**

The Risk

If no insurance is established here:

- The family faces funeral costs immediately
- Assets may be sold before they are passed on
- Grief becomes financial confusion
- Adult children may inherit stress instead of blessing

This is the stage where **love either leaves comfort or leaves chaos.**

Best Policy Strategy

Final Expense (Burial Insurance) + Survivorship (If Married) + Single Premium Life (If Savings Exist)

Policy	Role
Final Expense	Covers funeral & final costs so no burden falls on the family
Survivorship Life	Ensures children or grandchildren receive inheritance
Single Premium Life	Turns savings into a *tax-free gift* instead of taxable assets

Financial Reasoning

At this age:

- Cash may be available
- Income may be fixed
- Loans are difficult
- Coverage is harder to obtain

So the strategy must be:

- Simple
- Guaranteed
- Permanent

Legacy Purpose

This stage says:

"My love will take care of you even when I cannot."

It is the **final act of covering your family with grace.**

Section Completion Summary

Life Stage	Best Policy Type	Purpose
0–18	Juvenile Whole Life	Plant wealth foundation early
18–25	Convertible Term	Start protection at lowest cost
25–35	Term + Whole Life/IUL	Protect income + build generational wealth
35–55	Term + IUL/Whole Life	Preserve and expand legacy during peak earning years
55–69	GUL / Whole Life / Single Premium	Secure final lifetime coverage + transfer wealth efficiently
69+	Final Expense + Survivorship + Single Premium	

Chapter 30 — Life Insurance Is Legacy

This is where the truth gets real:

A good man leaves an inheritance to his children's children.
— Proverbs 13:22

This means:

- Your responsibility is not just to live well.
- Your responsibility is to **leave well.**

Life insurance is **the simplest, most accessible, most powerful tool** for generational wealth.

You don't have to be rich to leave something.
But you can leave something that will make your family more secure.

You can leave:

- Debt-free living

- Paid-off housing
- Funds for college
- Capital for business
- Stability during hardship
- Hope in a moment of grief

This is **how you break generational struggle.**

This is **how you build generational peace.**

This is **how you create legacy.**

Conclusion — Love Requires Action

If you love your family, protect them.
If you value your life, secure your legacy.
If you want your name to mean something after you are gone, plan for it.

This is not fear.
This is **responsibility.**

This is not preparation for death.
This is **preparation for life — their life.**

Do it today.
Not tomorrow.
Not later.
Not "when you get around to it."
Your family's future is too important.

Choose love.
Choose protection.
Choose legacy.

Get insured today!

Do **not** wait.

Life insurance gets **more expensive every year you age.**
And health can change at any moment.

Waiting costs:

- More money
- More stress
- More risk

Your family deserves better.

The best time to get life insurance was yesterday.

The second best time — **is right now.**

Your family will thank you —
Not now…
But when they need it the most.

Other Books by Rev. Darryl Bass

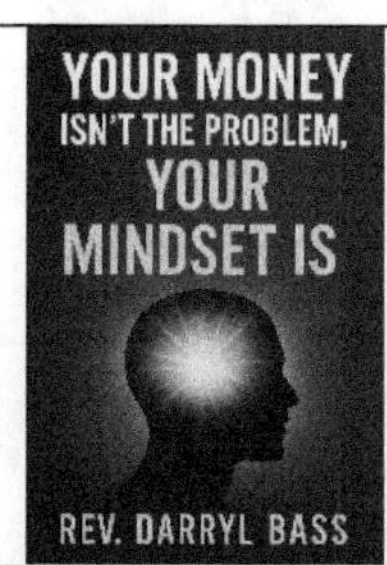	**Your Money Isn't the Problem, Your Mindset Is** A transformational work that challenges limiting financial beliefs and redefines wealth from the inside out, empowering readers to align their identity with abundance and responsibility.
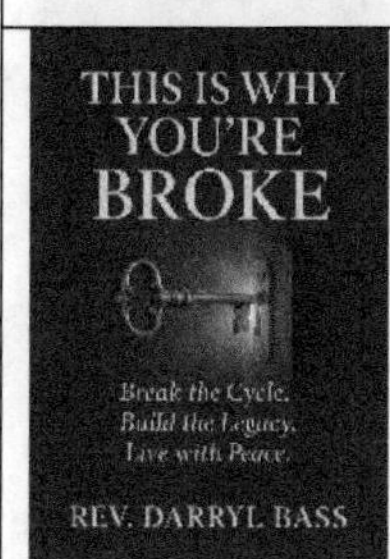	**This Is Why You're Broke** A bold and unapologetic examination of the habits, beliefs, and financial behaviors that keep people trapped in cycles of struggle. This book confronts uncomfortable truths and replaces excuses with execution, helping readers shift from reactive spending to strategic wealth building.

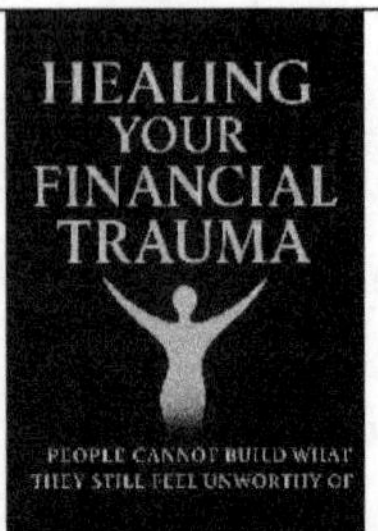 	**Healing Your Financial Trauma** This book addresses the psychological and emotional roots of money struggles, helping readers break cycles, confront financial pain, and rebuild confidence and stability.
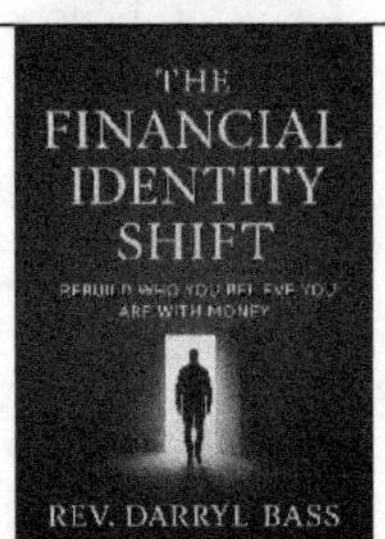 	**The Financial Identity Shift** A mindset-and-behavior reset that helps readers align who they are with how they handle money, transforming financial habits through identity-based discipline.
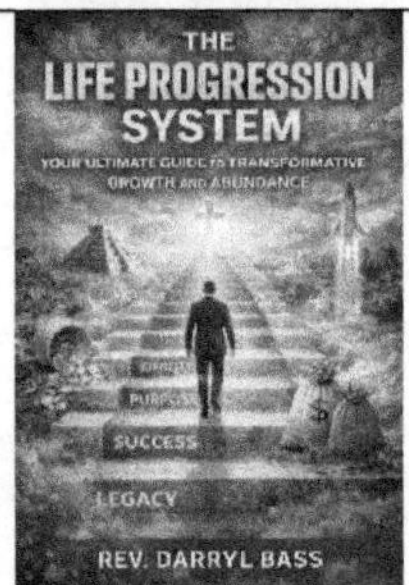 	**The Life Progression System** A comprehensive blueprint for intentional living, The Life Progression System guides readers through structured personal growth, goal alignment, mindset transformation, and legacy building. It equips individuals with practical tools to move from drifting through life to deliberately designing it.

<table>
<tr><td></td><td></td></tr>
<tr><td>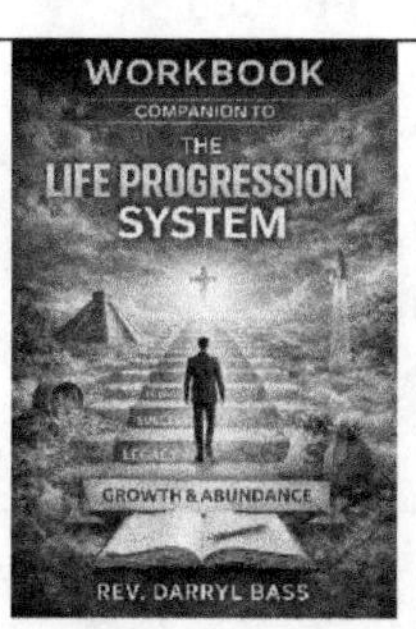
</td><td>The Life Progression System Workbook

A comprehensive blueprint for intentional living, The Life Progression System guides readers through structured personal growth, goal alignment, mindset transformation, and legacy building. It equips individuals with practical tools to move from drifting through life to deliberately designing it.</td></tr>
<tr><td></td><td></td></tr>
<tr><td>
</td><td>Financial Progression System

This book provides a step-by-step roadmap to financial stability and long-term wealth building. It teaches readers how to increase income, eliminate debt, build credit, create savings systems, and establish generational financial security.</td></tr>
<tr><td></td><td></td></tr>
</table>

<table>
<tr><td>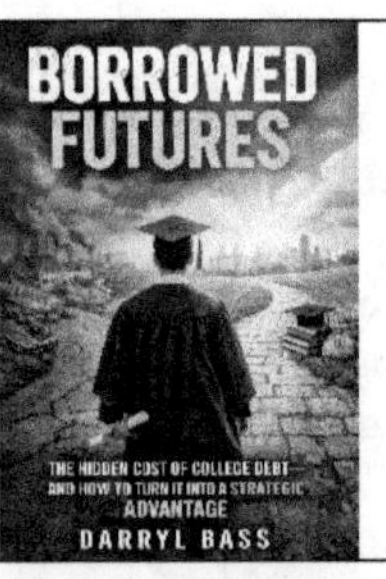</td><td>Borrowed Futures

A wake-up call about the hidden costs of debt and financial shortcuts, showing readers how to escape debt cycles and build futures without financial bondage.</td></tr>
<tr><td></td><td></td></tr>
<tr><td>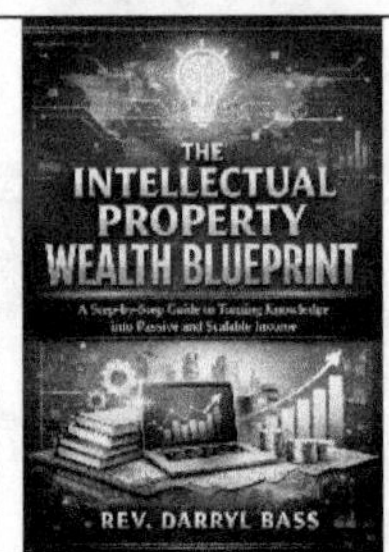</td><td>The Intellectual Property Wealth Blueprint

A strategic guide to turning knowledge into income, this book teaches creators how to package ideas into books, courses, systems, and assets that generate scalable and recurring revenue streams.</td></tr>
<tr><td></td><td></td></tr>
<tr><td>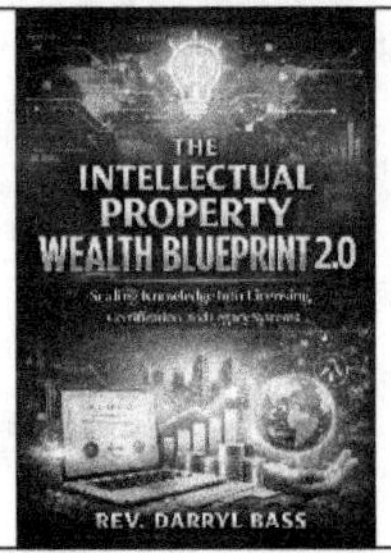</td><td>The Intellectual Property Wealth Blueprint 2.0
Focused on licensing, certification, and legacy systems, this volume expands intellectual property into scalable enterprises that create long-term wealth and generational ownership structures.</td></tr>
<tr><td></td><td></td></tr>
</table>

The Debt Eliminator
Coming 2026

What if 2026 was the year everything changed?

What if this was the year you stopped surviving… and started building?
The year you stopped juggling bills… and started creating wealth?
The year debt stopped controlling your decisions?

The **Debt Eliminator** is not another budgeting class.
It is a structured financial transformation system designed to help individuals and families break free from consumer debt, rebuild financial confidence, and establish a foundation for long-term wealth.

This course was built for hardworking people who are tired of living paycheck to paycheck. It was created for families who want stability, not stress.

It was designed for individuals who know they are capable of more—but need a system that works.

What the Debt Eliminator Will Teach You:

• How to eliminate consumer debt strategically and aggressively
• How to increase income without adding overwhelm
• How to rebuild and optimize your credit profile
• How to build savings while eliminating debt
• How to structure emergency funds and protection plans
• How to shift your financial identity from borrower to builder
• How to create systems that prevent debt from returning

This is not theory.
This is execution.

Through step-by-step modules, implementation tools, accountability structure, and real-life application, you will learn how to take control of your money instead of letting it control you.

Imagine waking up without financial anxiety.
Imagine having a plan.
Imagine watching your balances decrease and your confidence increase.
Imagine positioning your household for ownership, investing, and generational legacy.

That transformation begins in 2026.

The Debt Eliminator is more than a course.
It is a movement toward financial clarity, discipline, and freedom.

Get ready to break cycles.
Get ready to build stability.
Get ready to eliminate debt—permanently.

The Financial Freedom Revolution Tour
Launching 2026

This is not a seminar.
This is not a motivational rally.
This is a financial awakening.

The **Financial Freedom Revolution Tour** is a live, high-impact experience designed to ignite transformation in individuals, families, entrepreneurs, and communities ready to break financial cycles and build generational stability.

For too long, people have been working harder but falling further behind. Income rises. Expenses rise. Stress rises. Yet true financial progress feels out of reach.

The Revolution changes that.

This national tour brings together powerful teaching, real strategy, live coaching, and structured execution plans that move attendees from confusion to clarity—and from debt to disciplined wealth-building.

What You'll Experience:

- A clear roadmap to financial stability and long-term wealth
- Step-by-step strategies for eliminating consumer debt
- Income growth frameworks and entrepreneurship positioning
- Credit optimization and financial leverage strategies
- Protection planning and legacy-building principles
- Live financial assessments and actionable implementation steps
- A mindset shift from survival thinking to ownership thinking

This is not inspiration without structure.
This is strategy with accountability.

The Financial Freedom Revolution Tour is built for families who want peace instead of pressure. For entrepreneurs who want profit with structure.

For leaders who understand that financial stability is the foundation for community impact.

Imagine thousands gathered in one space—
learning, planning, committing to real change.
Imagine leaving with a clear blueprint instead of just excitement.
Imagine knowing exactly what steps to take the next day.

This is more than an event.
It is a declaration that debt cycles end here.
It is a call to financial responsibility, ownership, and generational leadership.

Cities across the country will host this movement in 2026.

Seats will fill.
Lives will shift.
Legacies will be built.

The Financial Freedom Revolution Tour — Coming 2026.

This is the year you stop reacting to money
…and start commanding it.

The revolution begins with one decision.

https://savingssolution.org/tour

Follow on Social Media

Facebook:

https://www.facebook.com/LPSCoach

Twitter:

https://twitter.com/LPS_Coach

Instagram:

https://www.instagram.com/lps_coach/

YouTube:

https://www.youtube.com/@life_progression_system

TikTok:

https://www.tiktok.com/@debt_annihilator

LinkedIn:

https://www.linkedin.com/in/lpscoach/

www.ingramcontent.com/pod-product-compliance
Lightning Source LLC
LaVergne TN
LVHW020713110826
845149LV00012B/2251

* 9 7 8 1 9 7 2 1 1 5 2 1 3 *